W9-AYO-189

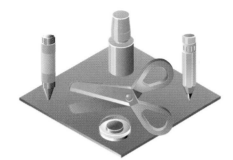

THE
CHILD'S
WORLD

HALLOWEEN CRAFTS

by Jean Eick

Library of Congress Cataloging-in-Publication Data
Eick, Jean. 1947-
Halloween Crafts / by Jean Eick.
p. cm.
Includes index.
Summary: Provides instructions for making spider
decorations, pumpkin cut-outs, masks, treat bags,
Halloween cards, and more.
ISBN 1-56766-535-7 (library bound : alk. Paper)

1. Halloween decorations — Juvenile literature.
2. Handicraft — Juvenile literature.
[1. Halloween decorations. 2. Handicraft.]
I. Title.
TT900.H32E33 1998   98-3247
745.594'1 — dc21   CIP
                                                           AC

GRAPHIC DESIGN & ILLUSTRATION
Robert A. Honey, Seattle

PRODUCTION COORDINATION
James R. Rothaus / James R. Rothaus & Associates

ELECTRONIC PRE-PRESS PRODUCTION
Robert E. Bonaker / Graphic Design & Consulting Company

CONTENTS

1 Halloween is a fun holiday full of scares and laughs. It's also a time for dressing up in costumes. Many people like to decorate for this special day, too. You can have fun making the Halloween crafts in this book all by yourself.

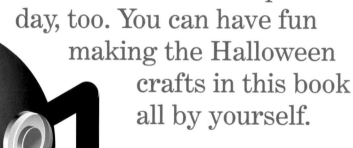

2 Before you start making any craft, be sure to read the directions. Make sure you look at the pictures too, they will help you understand what to do. Go through the list of things you'll need and get everything together. When you're ready, find a good place to work. Now you can begin making your crafts!

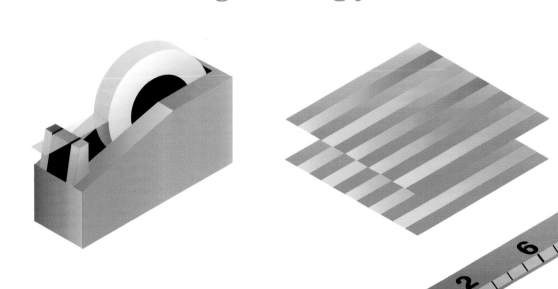

These spiders are cute, and creepy too! They make great decorations for your house or classroom.

SPIDERS

2 Movable Eyes..

4 Black Pipe Cleaners.

1 Large Black Pompon.

Glue.

1 Take two *black* pipe cleaners and wrap the middle of one around the middle of the other. (see example above.)

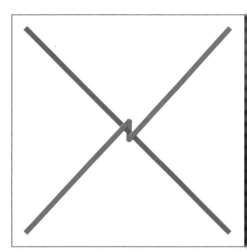

2 Do the same with the other two *black* pipe cleaners.

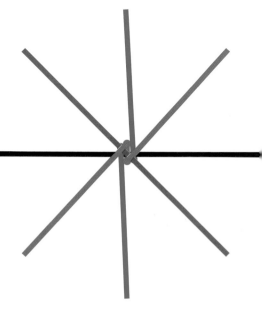

3 Wrap the two sets of pipe cleaners together.

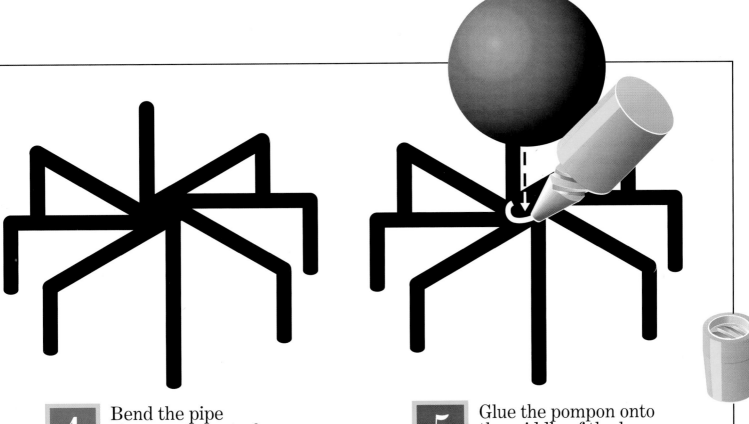

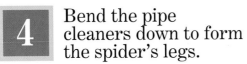
4 Bend the pipe cleaners down to form the spider's legs.

5 Glue the pompon onto the middle of the legs. Make sure you hold it until the glue sticks.

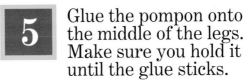

6 Glue the eyes on the front of the pompon. If you want, shape the legs of the spider some more.

*Paper pumpkins
are easy to make.
They are great for
decorating everything.*

PUMPKIN
CUTOUTS

Things
You'll Need

Scissors.

*Construction Paper:
1 Red.
1 Brown.
1 Black.*

Pencil.   *Glue.*

*1 Large Drinking Glass,
Coffee Cup, Or Cereal Bowl.*

1 Take the glass, cup, or bowl
and turn it over on the orange
piece of paper. Then
draw around the
edge to create
a circle.

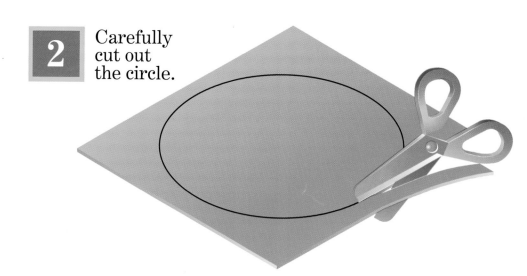

2 Carefully
cut out
the circle.

3

Draw a stem on the brown piece of paper and cut it out.

4

On the black piece of paper, draw some triangle shapes to use for the pumpkin's eyes, nose, and mouth. Then cut them out.

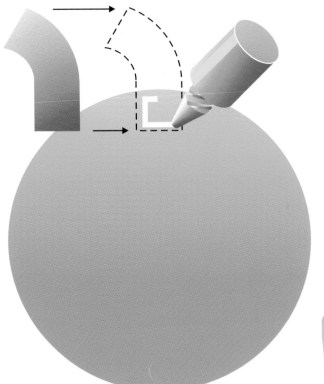

5 Glue the stem on the back of the orange circle.

6 Glue the triangles onto the front of the circle to make the pumpkin's face.

These easy masks are great for plays, and other special times too!

MASKS

Things You'll Need

Scissors.

A Large White Paper Plate.

Pencil.

Drinking Straw.

Glue.

Things for Decorating

Construction Paper.

Yarn Is Great.

Crayons.

Markers And Paint.

Stickers.

1 Take a paper plate, and draw the shape you want your mask to be. Choose any shape you want!

2 Carefully cut out the mask.

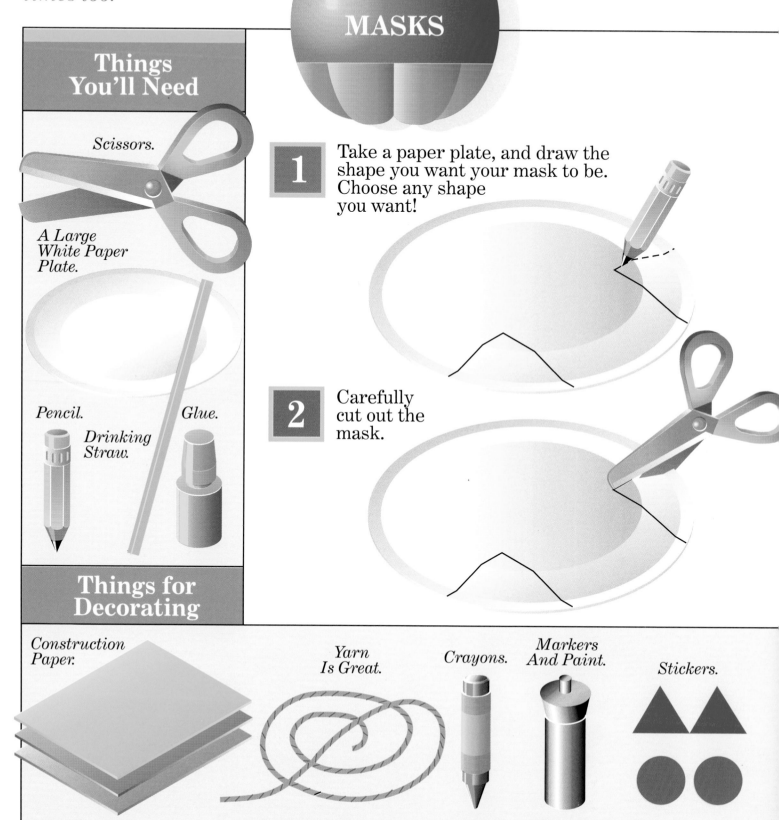

3 Hold the mask up to your face. Using the pencil, very lightly draw circles around your eyes.

Carefully cut out the eyes. **4**

5 Decorate the mask however you like. You can use yarn for silly beards, hair and eyebrows.

Construction paper and markers are great for making goofy mouths, noses, and other decorations. **6**

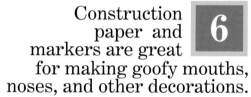

7 Glue the straw on the back of the mask.

When the glue is dry, your mask is ready. Use the straw as a handle to hold the mask in front of your face. **8**

Instead of carving pumpkins, try painting some faces on them. You can give them to special people as gifts.

PAINTED PUMPKINS

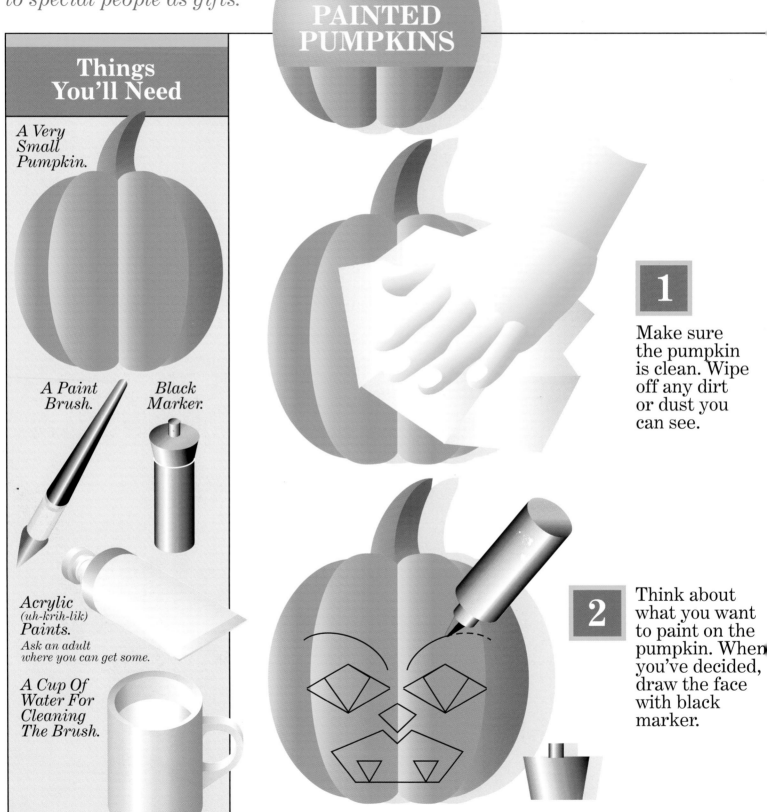

Things You'll Need

A Very Small Pumpkin.

A Paint Brush.

Black Marker.

Acrylic (uh-krih-lik) Paints. Ask an adult where you can get some.

A Cup Of Water For Cleaning The Brush.

1 Make sure the pumpkin is clean. Wipe off any dirt or dust you can see.

2 Think about what you want to paint on the pumpkin. When you've decided, draw the face with black marker.

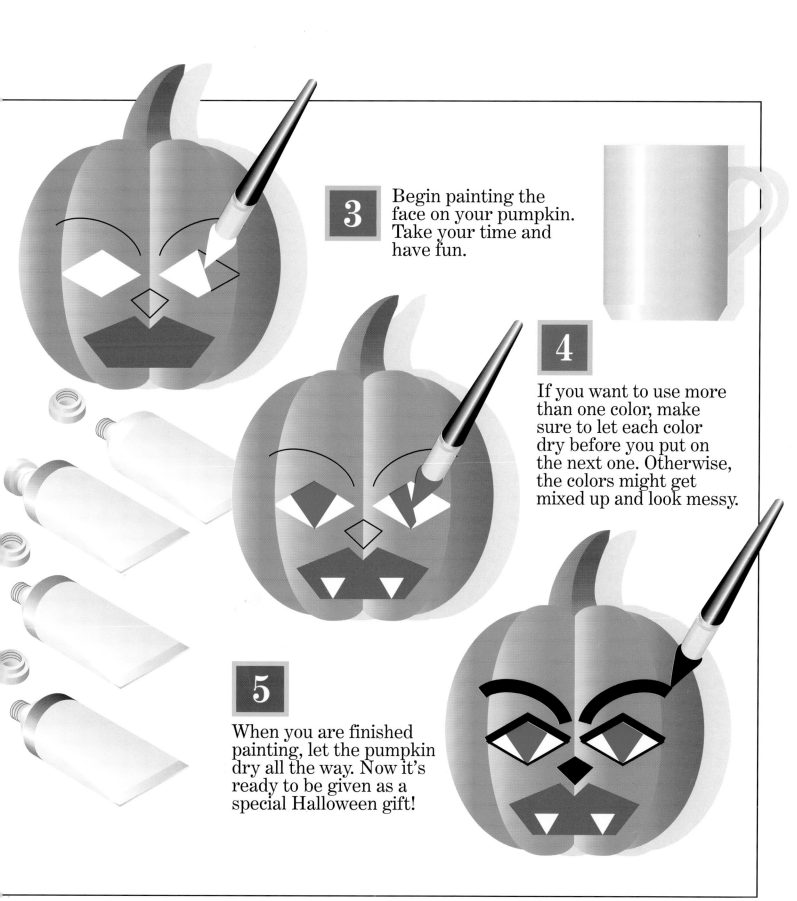

3 Begin painting the face on your pumpkin. Take your time and have fun.

4 If you want to use more than one color, make sure to let each color dry before you put on the next one. Otherwise, the colors might get mixed up and look messy.

5 When you are finished painting, let the pumpkin dry all the way. Now it's ready to be given as a special Halloween gift!

Make some of these bags as special Halloween gifts for your friends.

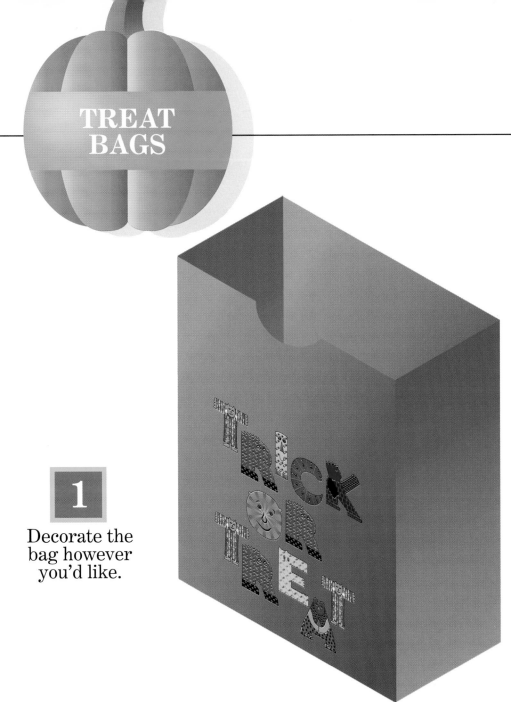

TREAT BAGS

Things You'll Need

Paper Lunch Bags.

Hole Puncher.

Yarn Is Great.

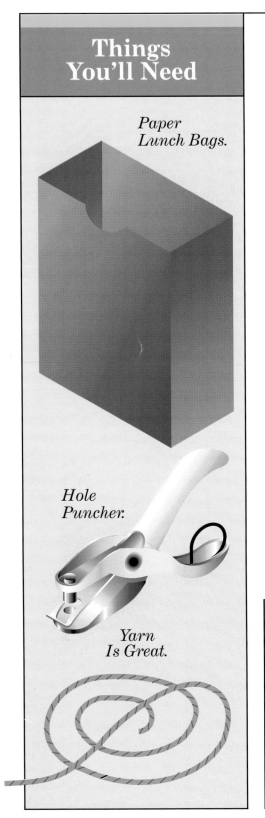

1

Decorate the bag however you'd like.

Things for Decorating

Markers. *Crayons.* *Stickers*

Glitter.

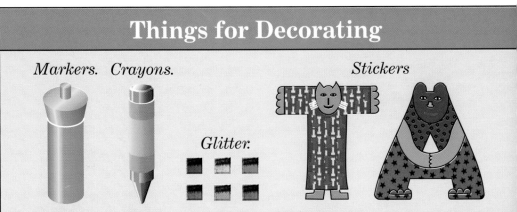

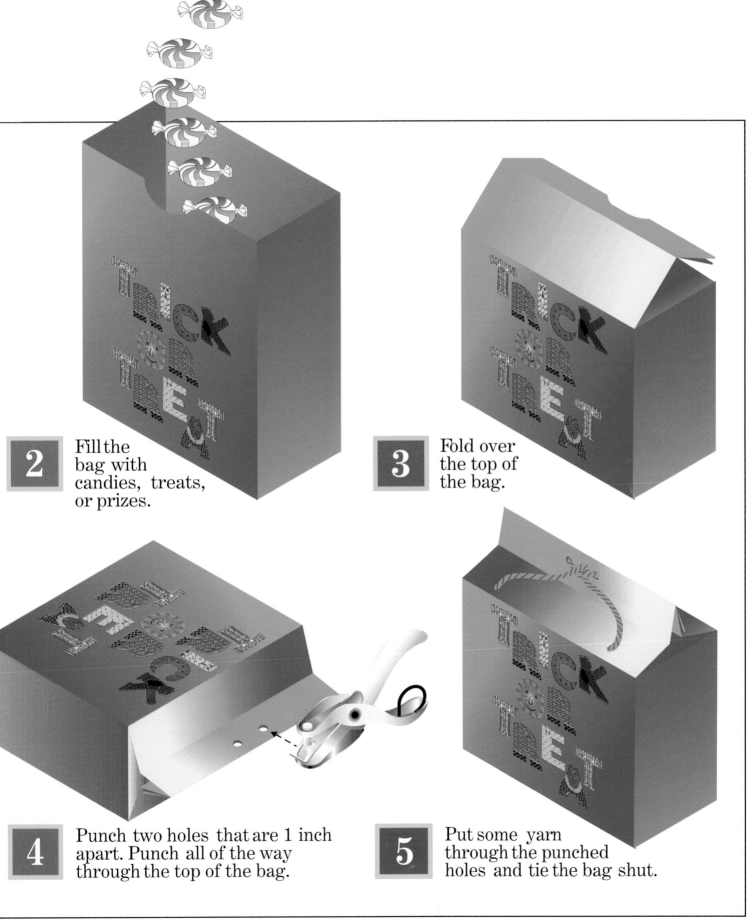

2 Fill the bag with candies, treats, or prizes.

3 Fold over the top of the bag.

4 Punch two holes that are 1 inch apart. Punch all of the way through the top of the bag.

5 Put some yarn through the punched holes and tie the bag shut.

Cards are a great way to say "Happy Halloween" to your grandparents, teachers, parents and friends.

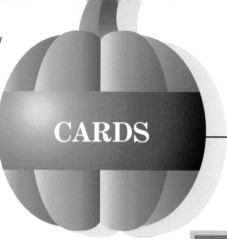

CARDS

1 Fold the paper to the size you want your card to be. Folding it once will make a large card.

2 Folding it twice will make a small card.

3 Decorate the front of the card.

4 Write a message on the inside of the card. You can decorate the inside, too. Don't forget to sign your name.

Things for Decorating

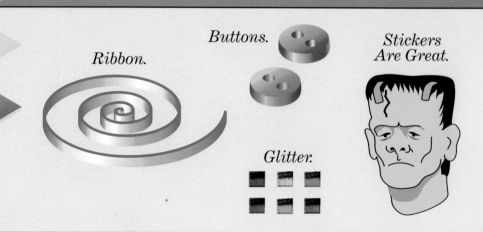

Ribbon.

Buttons.

Stickers Are Great.

Glitter.

You can make Halloween cards in many different ways.
Here are some ideas for making your cards even more special:

Draw lots of
spiders, ghosts,
and bats for a
spooky card.

2

Use black
construction
paper to make
your card. Then
use white crayons
to draw silly
ghosts.

Cut pictures
from magazines
to stick on
your card.
Bats, witches,
and the moon
are fun ideas.

You can even
make your own
envelopes to fit
your cards!

ENVELOPES

Things You'll Need

Scissors.

Construction Paper, Wrapping Paper, or Paper Bag.

Pencil.

Tape or Glue.

Ruler.

To make a square envelope

1 Cut out the front of a plain paper bag. It will take an 8 inch square piece of paper to hold a 5¼ inch square card.

2 Cut out a squar 8 inches high a 8 inches across. Measure and p an "X" in the center of the square.

3 Fold three of the corners so they cover the "X". Tape or glue the corners so they'll stay in place.

4 Place your card inside, then fold the top down and tape it shut.

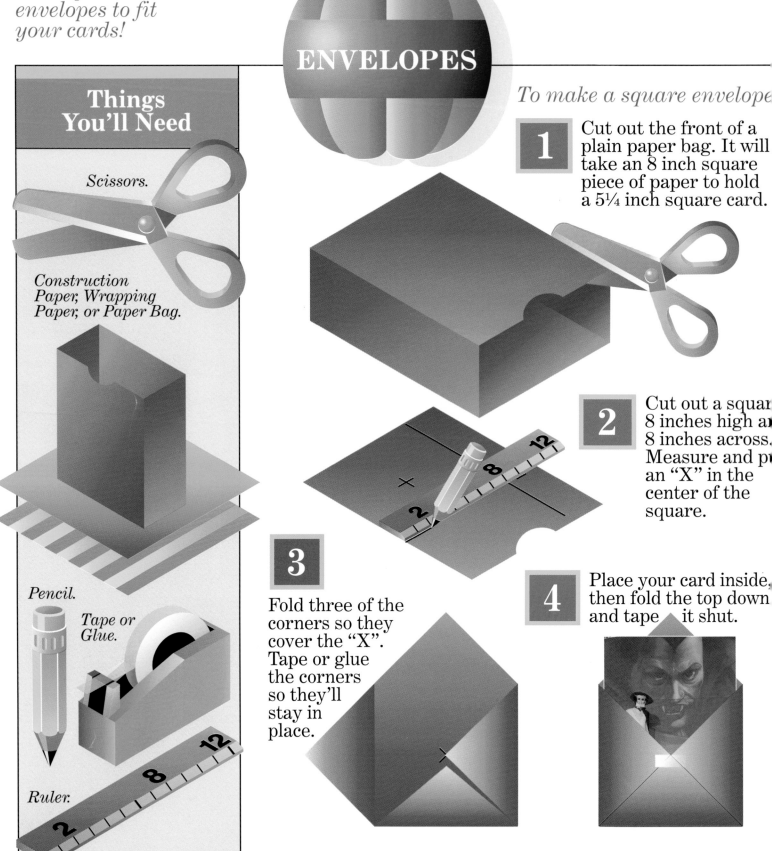

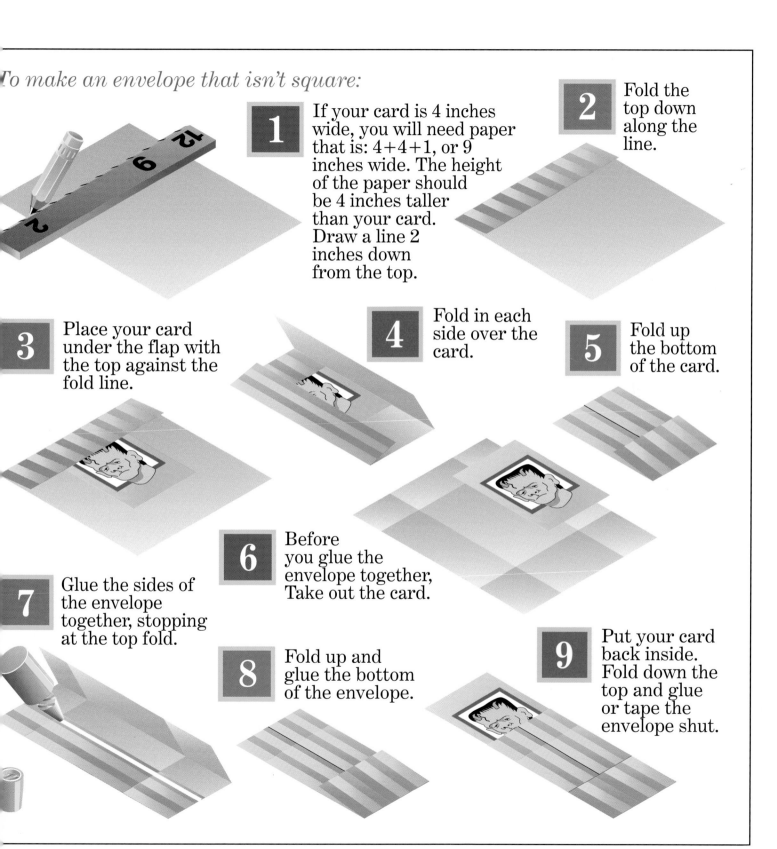

To make an envelope that isn't square:

1 If your card is 4 inches wide, you will need paper that is: 4+4+1, or 9 inches wide. The height of the paper should be 4 inches taller than your card. Draw a line 2 inches down from the top.

2 Fold the top down along the line.

3 Place your card under the flap with the top against the fold line.

4 Fold in each side over the card.

5 Fold up the bottom of the card.

6 Before you glue the envelope together, Take out the card.

7 Glue the sides of the envelope together, stopping at the top fold.

8 Fold up and glue the bottom of the envelope.

9 Put your card back inside. Fold down the top and glue or tape the envelope shut.

Halloween is a great time to invite your friends over for some fun activities. Here are some great ideas.

ACTIVITIES

1 Take turns with friends making silly or scary faces with face paints. You can also draw smaller things such as bats, pumpkins, and ghosts on your cheeks.

2 Hold a Halloween party. decorate the room with the decorations from this book. You can add some orange and black streamers, too. Invite your friends over to play games and have fun. Make sure everyone wears a costume!

3 Have a Halloween parade during the day. Tell your friends to come over in their costumes. Then put on a parade in your neighborhood.

4 Hold a scarecrow party. Have people bring old clothes for making the scarecrow. Then stuff it with straw and leaves.

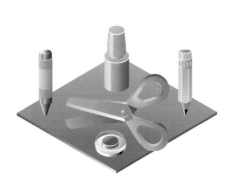